To read along, turn the page at the sound of the windchime.

To Susan, Elizabeth, and Scott,
who know how to imagine

Faith Kids® is an imprint of
Cook Communications Ministries,
Colorado Springs, Colorado 80918
Cook Communications, Paris, Ontario
Kingsway Communications, Eastbourne, England

SUN SONG
©2002 by Susan Scott Sutton for text and Sally Randall for illustrations

Library of Congress Cataloging-in-Publication Data

Sutton, Susan 1957-
    Sun song / Susan Scott Sutton ; illustrated by Sally Randall.
        p. cm.
    Summary: A lullaby in which a child goes to bed with a prayer of thanks after playing
    with the sun, wind, or rain that God has used to warm, sweep, or wash the earth and sky
    that day.
    ISBN 0-7814-3561-7
    1. Lullabies. 2. Children's songs. [1. God--Songs and music. 2. Lullabies. 3. Songs.]
    I. Randall, Sally, ill. II. Title.
    PZ8.3.S9916 Su 2002
    782.4215'82'0268--dc21

                                                        2001023416

First printing, 2002
Printed in Singapore
1 2 3 4 5 6 7 8 9 10 Printing/Year 06 05 04 03 02

Songwriter: Lynn Hodges
Editor: Heather Gemmen
Designer: Sally Randall

Sun Song

Written by Susan Scott Sutton
Illustrated by Sally Randall
Music by Lynn Hodges

Faith Parenting Guide found on page 28

I woke to the song of
the sun today;
he smiled and called
me out to play.

"Come away," he

said, "away."

8

We played all day, the sun and I,
while God was warming the earth and sky.
Racing in fields of flowers that sway,
chasing a mouse to his home in the hay,
finding in clouds a ship at bay.

9

It was an, oh, so marvelous day
for me, for me, for me...
a day for the sun and me.

I woke to the sigh of the wind today;
he swirled and called me out to play.

"Come away," he said, "away."

We played all day, the wind and I,
while God was sweeping the earth and the sky,
whirling and twirling the leaves up high,
dropping them down to the earth with a sigh,
whispering tales from heaven on high.

It was an, oh, so
splendid day
for me, for me, for me...
a day for the
wind and me.

I woke to the dance
of the rain today;
she skipped and
called me out to play.

"Come

away,"

she

said,

"away."

18

We played all day, the rain and I,
while God was washing the earth and the sky,
shaking the beads from the leaves of a tree,
sailing the boats on the edge of a sea,
leaping in oceans as high as my knee.

21

It was an, oh, so wonderful day,
for me, for me, for me...
a day for the rain and me.

22

I go to bed at the end of each day,
sun and wind and rain away.
Only the moon is out to play,
calling all children
to stop and pray,

"Give thanks to God for his work in the day."

24

26

God watches his world
so carefully,
and I am glad
because, you see,
there is no one awake
in the house but me,
but me, but me, but me...
but God, his angels, and me.

27

Sun Song

Life Issue: My children need to enjoy and thank God for the wonders of creation.

Spiritual Building Block: Thankfulness

Help your children learn about thankfulness in the following ways:

Nurture your children's God-given delight in creation by taking them on a leisurely walk through a lovely neighborhood or park, or along a country lane or shoreline.

Sight: Ask your children to look for, and then point out, interesting things that God has created. Challenge them to find as many as possible. Then ask your children to tell you what caused them to notice those things: Was it their color? Their shape? Their size? As you walk, conversationally thank the Lord for the special things you see.

Sound: At bedtime that night, ask your children to recreate the sounds you heard during your walk. Take turns thanking God for all the things you saw outside today. If you find yourself laughing, thank him for that too!

Touch: After you get home, help your children create a picture of what was most memorable about the walk, whether it was the sights, sounds, textures, or smells. Or, if they brought home mementos from the walk — such as leaves, flowers, or interesting rocks — encourage them to create a shoe-box display case. Then help them choose a Bible verse about God's creation to be written on the picture or display case.

Susan Scott Sutton is a missionary in Chad with Worldwide Evangelization for Christ. Her husband Louis does medical ministry, while Susan concentrates on women's evangelism. Susan and Louis have three teenagers.

Sally Randall lives with her husband and two sons in Colorado Springs, Colorado. Illustrating this book has been the opportunity to combine two passions: her heart for God and her heart to reach children through art with the unfailing love of an unfailing Savior.

Lynn Hodges is a professor of music, voice, music theory and piano. She has had multiple nominations for the Gospel Music Association's Dove awards. She lives with her husband and three children in Nashville, TN.

Equipping Kids for Life
faithkids.com